Level 5 - ⑥

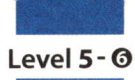

The Story of the Reformation

Joseph Poulshock

Series Editor **Rob Waring**

Level 5 - ❻

The Story of the Reformation

Joseph Poulshock

© 2017 Seed Learning, Inc.

Series Editor: Rob Waring
Acquisitions Editor: Liana Robinson
Copy Editor: Casey Malarcher
Cover/Interior Design: Andy Roh

ISBN: 978-1-9464-5245-0

10 9 8 7 6 5 4 3 2 1
21 20 19 18 17

John Wycliffe

W ho was this dead man? What did he do, and why is he important? The man was John Wycliffe (1330–1384). He was one of the first men to try to change religion in Europe. It was a big change called the Reformation, and people like Wycliffe were called reformers.

Six hundred years ago, the Roman Catholic Church had great power in Europe. Although Wycliffe was a leader in the Catholic Church in England, he also spoke against the Catholic Church. He thought that some changes should be made.

John Wycliffe

A Roman Catholic Church in Florence, Italy

The Morning Star of the Reformation

During Wycliffe's time, the Roman Catholic Church worshiped in Latin even though not everyone understood it. Throughout Europe, all Christian Bibles were in Latin, too. Wycliffe, who lived in England, spoke English and Latin.

Wycliffe wanted people to be able to read the Bible in English, so he translated it. The church leaders in Rome did not like this or his teachings.

Wycliffe also wrote books that challenged the church to reform. He is often called "The Morning Star of the Reformation." Church leaders burned Wycliffe's writings. But Wycliffe's ideas did not disappear. They influenced other reformers.

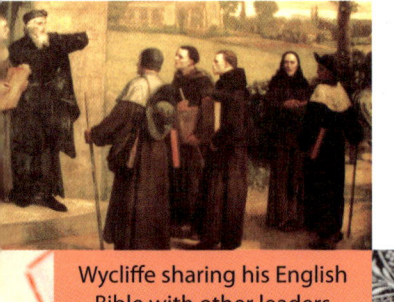

Wycliffe sharing his English Bible with other leaders

SANCTUM IESU CHRISTI EVANGELIUM SECUNDUM IOANNEM

Prologus evangelistæ,

A Latin Bible

principio 6 erat verbum, et verbum era, um, et Deus erat verbum. 2 Hoc in

Getting Back to Roots

There were other reformers like John Wycliffe. They started to reform the church, too. During the Renaissance, thinkers looked back at the great cultures of Greece and Rome. Renaissance thinkers wanted to learn from the past. Church reformers, too, wanted to learn from their Christian roots in the years just after Jesus died. They wanted to follow the Bible, which was written between 50–100 A.D.

A church window with Wycliffe in the center, surrounded by the names of other reformers

The early teachings were very different from those in the Roman Catholic Church. The Roman Catholic Church told its people to follow many traditions that the early church did not do, and ones not written in the Bible. The reformers didn't like these traditions.

Wycliffe on trial for his ideas

Luther and the Protestants

Martin Luther

Another reformer who lived after Wycliff was a German called Martin Luther (1483–1546). Like Wycliffe, Luther was a leader in the Catholic Church. And he saw many problems in the church.

For example, Catholics believed that God would punish them for doing bad things. But the Roman Catholic Church made a way to reduce this punishment. If a Catholic person bought an "indulgence," the Pope said that God would forgive them or reduce the punishment.

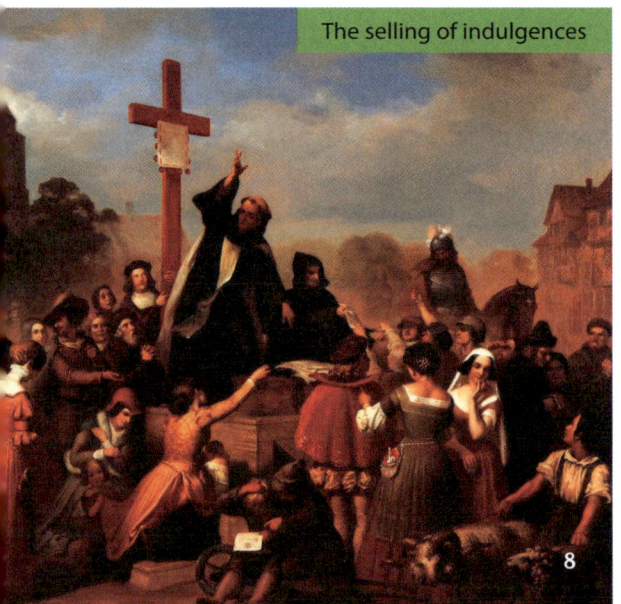

The selling of indulgences

But this practice was not in the Bible, and it became misused. The Catholic Church sold indulgences to get money. The Catholic Church was selling God's forgiveness.

8

The Ninety-Five Theses

Luther was a scholar, and he carefully studied this problem. Then he wrote a paper against the practice of selling indulgences. This paper called the "Ninety-Five Theses," gave 95 reasons why indulgences were bad.

The door at the Wittenberg Church

On October 31, 1517, Luther sent the Ninety-Five Theses to a leader of the church in Germany. In this way, Luther intended to discuss problems in the Roman Catholic Church. His theses were not hostile. Later in November, the work was translated into German and circulated.

Today, we call the Reformation the Protestant Reformation.

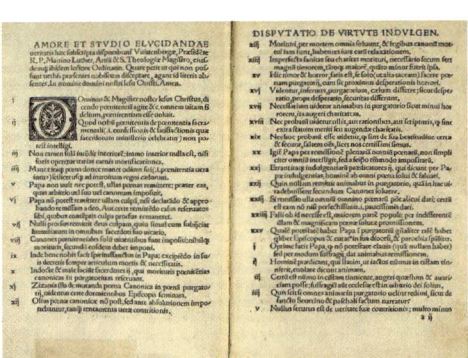

And October 31, 1517, is generally considered the beginning of the Protestant Reformation.

The first page of Luther's 95 theses

More Trouble Begins

Luther wanted to reform the Catholic Church, but church leaders did not want his advice. In April 1521, they ordered Luther to appear before a group of powerful leaders to explain his writings.

Luther defending himself

The man in charge of the meetings was Johann Eck. At the meeting, Eck asked Luther a hard question. He asked Luther if he would defend all his writings or reject some of them.

Luther, however, didn't give a yes or no answer. He gave a speech, trying to explain his ideas.

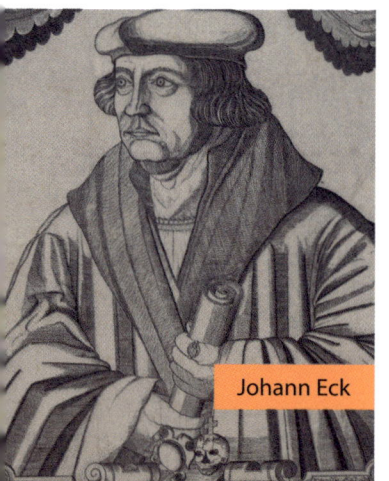
Johann Eck

Eck didn't want a speech. He wanted a simple answer. When Luther finished talking, Eck asked him the same question again. Did Luther reject his writings and his errors?

Luther Escapes

Luther basically said:

> *With my sense of right and wrong, I must follow the Word of God. I cannot change my mind. It is not safe to act against one's sense of right and wrong. God help me. Amen.*

In the days after the meeting, Eck and the other leaders decided Luther's punishment. The leaders ordered the burning of Luther's books and took his property. They called him an outlaw and a heretic.

Luther's life was in danger, but he was able to escape. He went into hiding.

Wartburg Castle, where Luther went into hiding

Luther's books are burned.

11

Martin Luther escaping

Frederick the Wise sent men to kidnap Luther. These men secretly took Luther to a safe place called Wartburg Castle.

Luther stayed at Wartburg Castle for about a year. During that time, he worked hard. He translated the Bible into common German, just like Wycliffe did for English. And he worked on many other books and writings in the quiet of the castle.

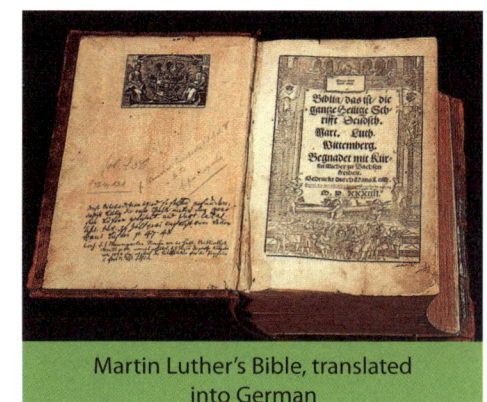

Martin Luther's Bible, translated into German

Culture and Conflict

Outside the castle, life was not quiet. Luther kept in contact with his supporters through letters. He and others challenged the power of the Roman Catholic Church.

Though still under threat of arrest, Luther secretly returned to Wittenberg in 1522. In his absence, other reformers had cropped up. There were many opinions and beliefs now involved in the opposition of the Catholic Church. Luther came out of hiding in order to set his followers straight.

Meanwhile, poor farmers called peasants were inspired by the Reformation. They saw Protestants breaking free from Roman Catholic oppression just as they themselves wanted to break free from the oppression of nobles and landlords.

A painting of peasant farmers gathering a crop (Millet, 1857)

A painting of peasant farmers praying (Millet, 1857)

The Peasants' War (1524-1525)

In 1524, peasants in Germany began to fight against nobles and landowners. The war began with separate revolts. In the beginning, there were some clear victories for the peasants.

However, the war quickly gathered steam. At its height, the war involved about 300,000 peasants.

The nobles had better armies, weapons, and funding. The peasants, many of whom had never fought before, found themselves fighting true soldiers. The peasants could not compete with the nobles. In the end, about 100,000 peasants were killed.

Peasants ready for war

John Calvin: The Organizer

Young John Calvin

After Luther, there were other important reformers. John Calvin was a Frenchman who worked in Geneva, Switzerland. In Geneva, Calvin took the ideas of Luther and other reformers, and he organized them. He made a system of teachings about the Reformation.

Calvin communicated these ideas very clearly. Reformers from all over Europe came to Geneva to learn from him. In time, the ideas of the Reformation spread all around Europe.

In Geneva, Calvin established a religious government. In 1555, he was the top leader in Geneva.

Calvin just before he died

Today, Calvin is viewed as one of the most important leaders of the Reformation.

15

For Church and Nation

John Wycliffe

Wycliffe, Luther, and Calvin wanted to return to the roots of the Christian faith. They wanted to reform the Roman Catholic Church. However, Wycliffe was English, Luther was German, and Calvin was French. By speaking against the Catholic Church, they were also showing their national spirit.

Even though they loved their own countries, reformers like Wycliffe, Luther, and Calvin loved the Roman Catholic Church. They saw problems in the church, and they worked within to change it. But when the church rejected them, the reformers were forced to start new churches.

A statue of Martin Luther

A Big Movement in History

These new churches were called Protestant churches. Today, the Roman Catholic Church is still the biggest church in the world, with 1.2 billion followers. But there are about 900 million Protestants in the world today. Clearly, with these numbers, we can see that the Protestant

The Saint Pierre Church in Geneva, where Calvin spoke

Reformation was a very big movement in human history.

Like Renaissance thinkers, reformers wanted to better understand where they came from. They wanted to more clearly understand and follow the first sources of their faith. When they did this, it greatly changed the shape of European history and the world.

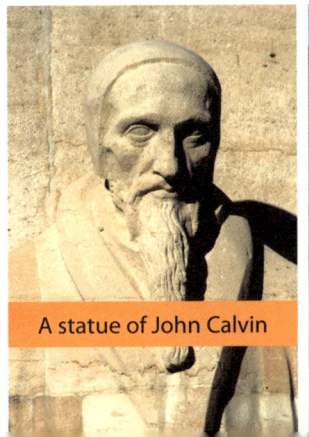

A statue of John Calvin

Statues of reformers

17

Comprehension Questions

1. John Wycliffe was from...
   - (a) Germany.
   - (b) England.
   - (c) France.
   - (d) Italy.

2. Whose bones were burned 44 years after he died?
   - (a) Luther
   - (b) Calvin
   - (c) Eck
   - (d) Wycliffe

3. Catholic Church leaders were angry at Wycliffe because he...
   - (a) spoke against the church.
   - (b) was a liar.
   - (c) loved money.
   - (d) was not religious.

4. Wycliffe translated the Bible from...
   - (a) English into Latin.
   - (b) Latin into English.
   - (c) Latin into German.
   - (d) German into French.

5. Martin Luther was from...
   - (a) Germany.
   - (b) England.
   - (c) France.
   - (d) Italy.

6. Luther wrote against the selling of indulgences in his...
   - (a) Bible.
   - (b) 95 theses.
   - (c) 66 books.
   - (d) 88 reasons.

7. Which was NOT one of Luther's punishments?
   - (a) His books were burned.
   - (b) His property was taken.
   - (c) He was put to death.
   - (d) He was cut off from the church.

8. Luther translated the Bible into common...
   - (a) English.
   - (b) Latin.
   - (c) German.
   - (d) French.

9. John Calvin was French, but he lived in...
   - (a) Rome.
   - (b) Geneva.
   - (c) London.
   - (d) Wittenberg.

10. What was the main goal of the reformers?
    - (a) To criticize Catholics
    - (b) To return to their roots
    - (c) To love each other
    - (d) To make money

Key 1. (b) 2. (d) 3. (a) 4. (b) 5. (a) 6. (b) 7. (c) 8. (c) 9. (b) 10. (b)

Glossary

- **Bible** the holy books of the Christian religion

- **castle** a large, strong building strengthened against attack, often where a king or queen lives

- **Catholic** concerning a Christian church organization based in Rome, Italy, and led by the Pope

- **hostile** not friendly; showing opposition to something

- **indulgence** the paying of money for forgiveness of a sin so you can more easily go to heaven

- **Latin** the language used by ancient Romans

- **peasant** a poor farmer

- **protest** to speak or act against something

- **Protestant** a member of one of the Christian churches that separated from the Roman Catholic Church

- **punish** to make someone suffer for doing something wrong

- **Renaissance** a time between the 14th and 17th centuries when people looked back at the teachings of the ancient Greeks and Romans

- **reject** to say no to something

- **tradition** a way of thinking or acting that is common in a culture

- **translate** to change words or ideas from one language to another

World History Timeline

This chart shows a rough overview of world history.
Some of the dates have been simplified.

World History Timeline

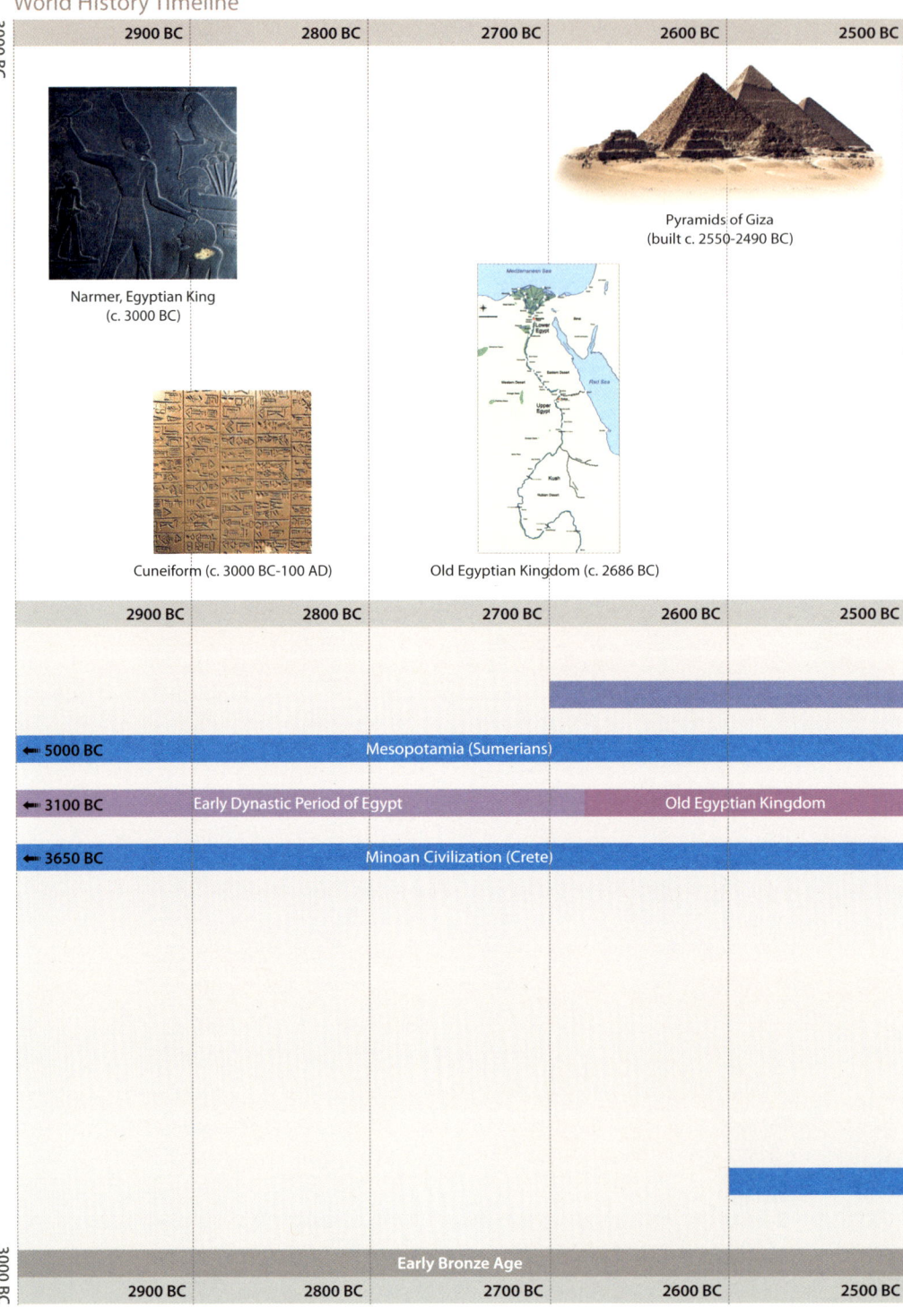

| 3000 BC | 2900 BC | 2800 BC | 2700 BC | 2600 BC | 2500 BC |

Narmer, Egyptian King
(c. 3000 BC)

Pyramids of Giza
(built c. 2550-2490 BC)

Cuneiform (c. 3000 BC-100 AD)

Old Egyptian Kingdom (c. 2686 BC)

| 2900 BC | 2800 BC | 2700 BC | 2600 BC | 2500 BC |

← 5000 BC Mesopotamia (Sumerians)

← 3100 BC Early Dynastic Period of Egypt — Old Egyptian Kingdom

← 3650 BC Minoan Civilization (Crete)

Early Bronze Age

| 3000 BC | 2900 BC | 2800 BC | 2700 BC | 2600 BC | 2500 BC |

2400 BC	2300 BC	2200 BC	2100 BC	2000 BC

Sahure, Egyptian King
(c. 2487-2475 BC)

Indus Valley
Civilization

Sargon the Great,
Akkadian King
(c. 2340-2284 BC)

Gudea of Lagash
(c. 2144-2124 BC)

Ur III Dynasty (c. 2112-2004 BC)

2400 BC	2300 BC	2200 BC	2100 BC	2000 BC

Xia Dynasty

Gutian Dynasty

Elam (Iran)

Akkadian Empire

Ur III Dynasty

Assyria (Early Period)

Middle Egyptian Kingdom

Minoan Civilization (Crete)

1st Intermediate
Period

Indus Valley Civilization (India)

2400 BC	2300 BC	2200 BC	2100 BC	2000 BC

World History Timeline

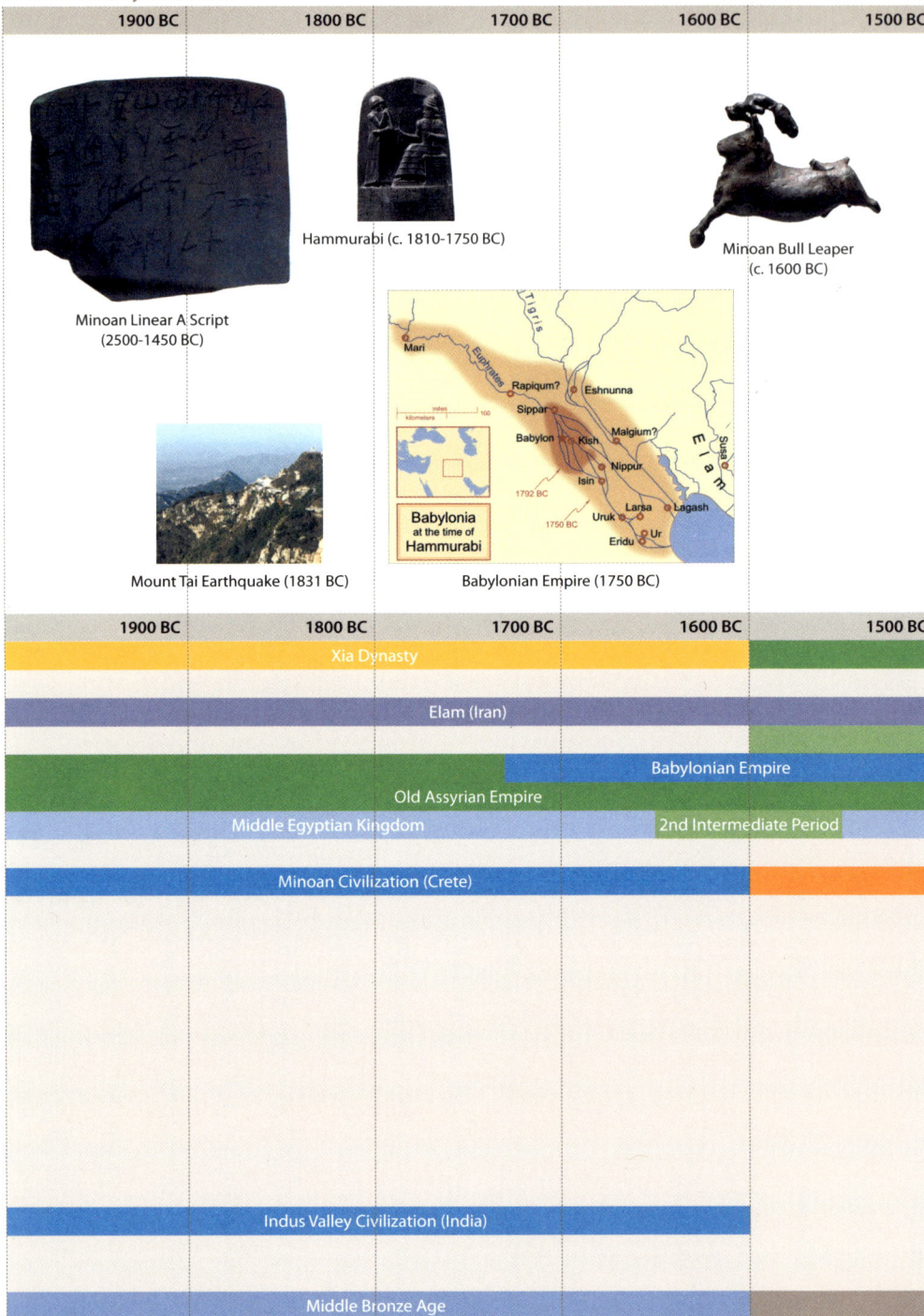

1900 BC	1800 BC	1700 BC	1600 BC	1500 BC

Minoan Linear A Script
(2500-1450 BC)

Hammurabi (c. 1810-1750 BC)

Minoan Bull Leaper
(c. 1600 BC)

Mount Tai Earthquake (1831 BC)

Babylonia
at the time of
Hammurabi

Babylonian Empire (1750 BC)

1900 BC	1800 BC	1700 BC	1600 BC	1500 BC

Xia Dynasty

Elam (Iran)

Babylonian Empire

Old Assyrian Empire

Middle Egyptian Kingdom

2nd Intermediate Period

Minoan Civilization (Crete)

Indus Valley Civilization (India)

Middle Bronze Age

1900 BC	1800 BC	1700 BC	1600 BC	1500 BC

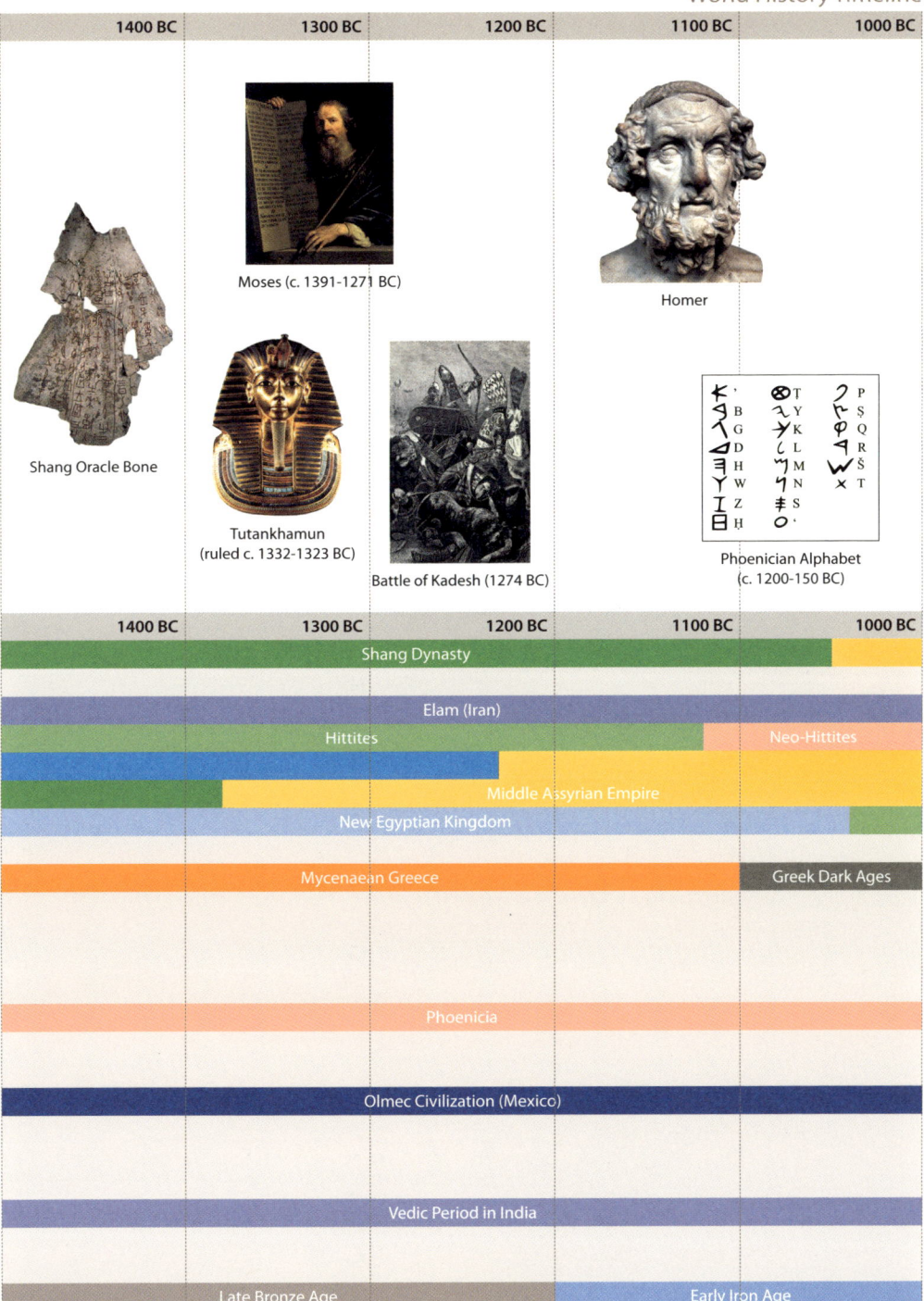

1400 BC	1300 BC	1200 BC	1100 BC	1000 BC

Shang Oracle Bone

Moses (c. 1391-1271 BC)

Tutankhamun (ruled c. 1332-1323 BC)

Battle of Kadesh (1274 BC)

Homer

Phoenician Alphabet (c. 1200-150 BC)

1400 BC	1300 BC	1200 BC	1100 BC	1000 BC

Shang Dynasty

Elam (Iran)

Hittites

Neo-Hittites

Middle Assyrian Empire

New Egyptian Kingdom

Mycenaean Greece

Greek Dark Ages

Phoenicia

Olmec Civilization (Mexico)

Vedic Period in India

Late Bronze Age

Early Iron Age

1400 BC	1300 BC	1200 BC	1100 BC	1000 BC

World History Timeline

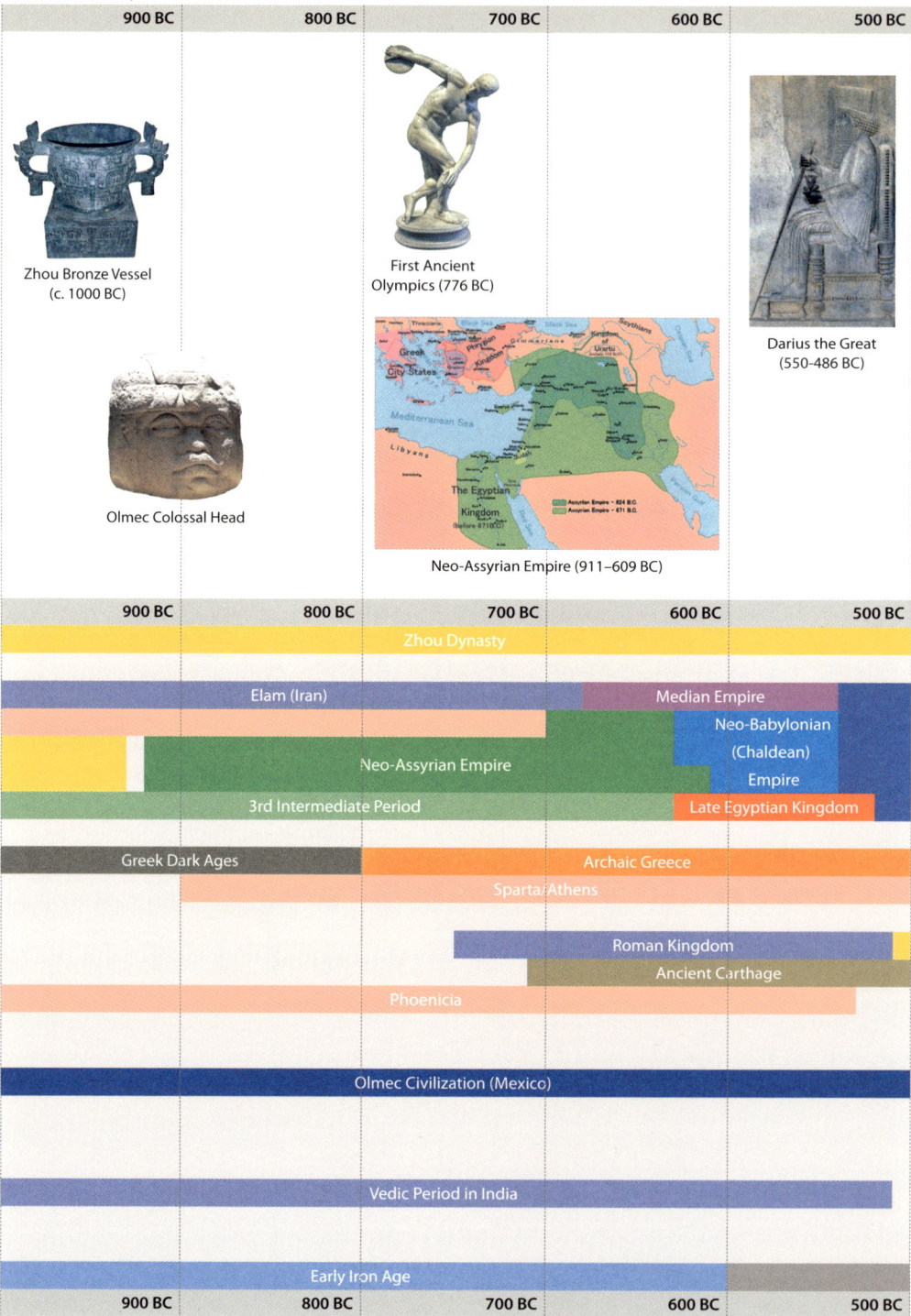

900 BC	800 BC	700 BC	600 BC	500 BC

Zhou Bronze Vessel
(c. 1000 BC)

First Ancient
Olympics (776 BC)

Olmec Colossal Head

Darius the Great
(550-486 BC)

Neo-Assyrian Empire (911–609 BC)

900 BC	800 BC	700 BC	600 BC	500 BC

Zhou Dynasty

Elam (Iran)

Median Empire

Neo-Babylonian (Chaldean) Empire

Neo-Assyrian Empire

3rd Intermediate Period

Late Egyptian Kingdom

Greek Dark Ages

Archaic Greece

Sparta/Athens

Roman Kingdom

Ancient Carthage

Phoenicia

Olmec Civilization (Mexico)

Vedic Period in India

Early Iron Age

900 BC	800 BC	700 BC	600 BC	500 BC

World History Timeline

| 400 BC | 300 BC | 200 BC | 100 BC | 0 |

Alexander the Great (356-323 BC)

Hannibal (247-183 BC)

Julius Caesar (100-44 BC)

Cleopatra (69-30 BC)

Battle of Salamis (480 BC)

Seleucid Empire (312-63 BC)

Rossetta Stone (created 196 BC)

| 400 BC | 300 BC | 200 BC | 100 BC | 0 |

Zhou Dynasty

Qin

Han Dynasty

Achaemenid (Persian) Empire

Alexander the Great

Parthian Empire

Seleucid Empire
Ptolemaic Kingdom
(Hellenistic Greece)

Classical Greece

Sparta/Athens

Roman Empire

Roman Republic

Roman Empire

Maurya Empire

Middle Iron Age

| 400 BC | 300 BC | 200 BC | 100 BC | 0 |

World History Timeline

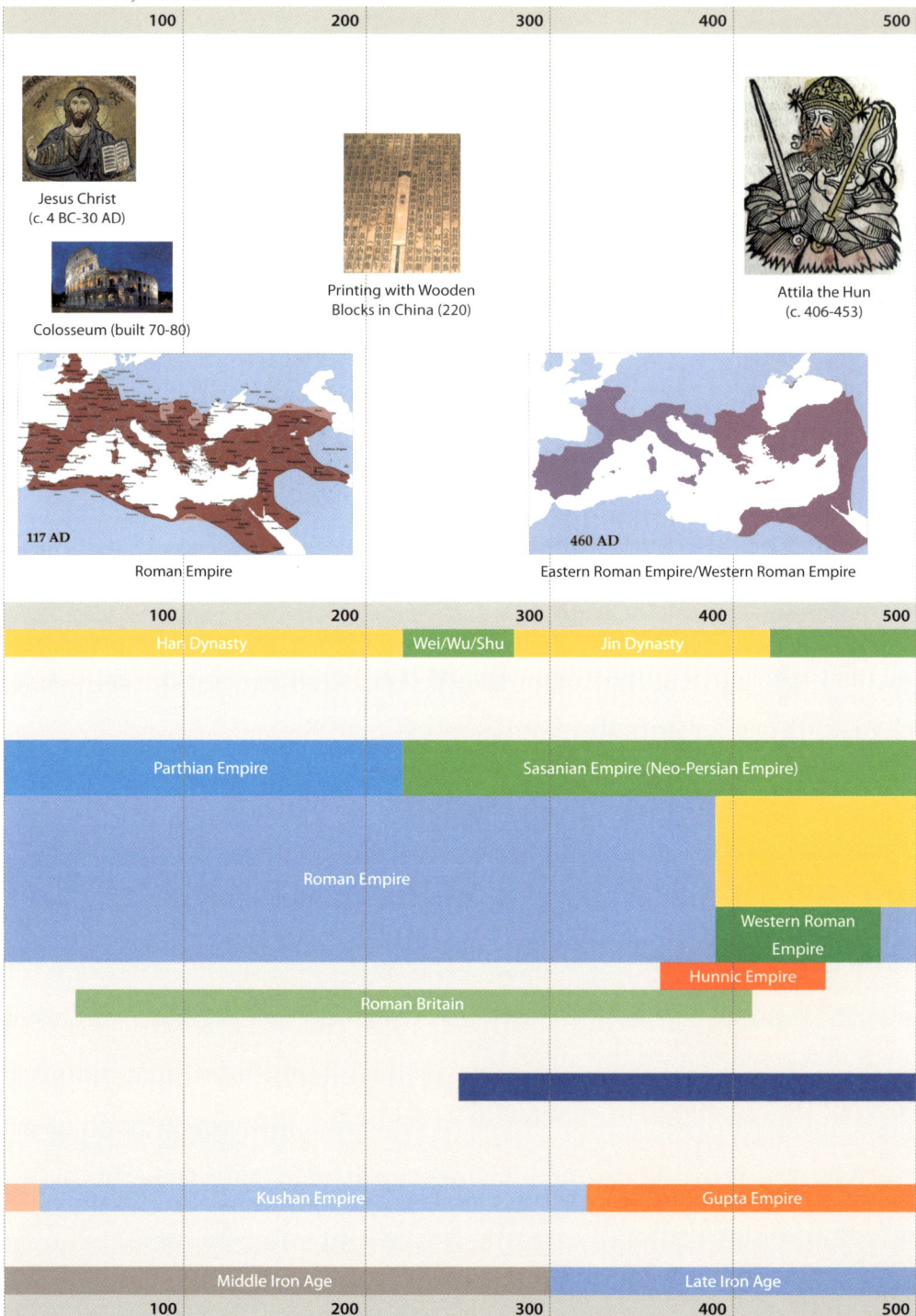

| | 100 | 200 | 300 | 400 | 500 |

Jesus Christ
(c. 4 BC-30 AD)

Printing with Wooden
Blocks in China (220)

Attila the Hun
(c. 406-453)

Colosseum (built 70-80)

117 AD

Roman Empire

460 AD

Eastern Roman Empire/Western Roman Empire

| | 100 | 200 | 300 | 400 | 500 |

Han Dynasty

Wei/Wu/Shu

Jin Dynasty

Parthian Empire

Sasanian Empire (Neo-Persian Empire)

Roman Empire

Western Roman Empire

Hunnic Empire

Roman Britain

Kushan Empire

Gupta Empire

Middle Iron Age

Late Iron Age

| | 100 | 200 | 300 | 400 | 500 |

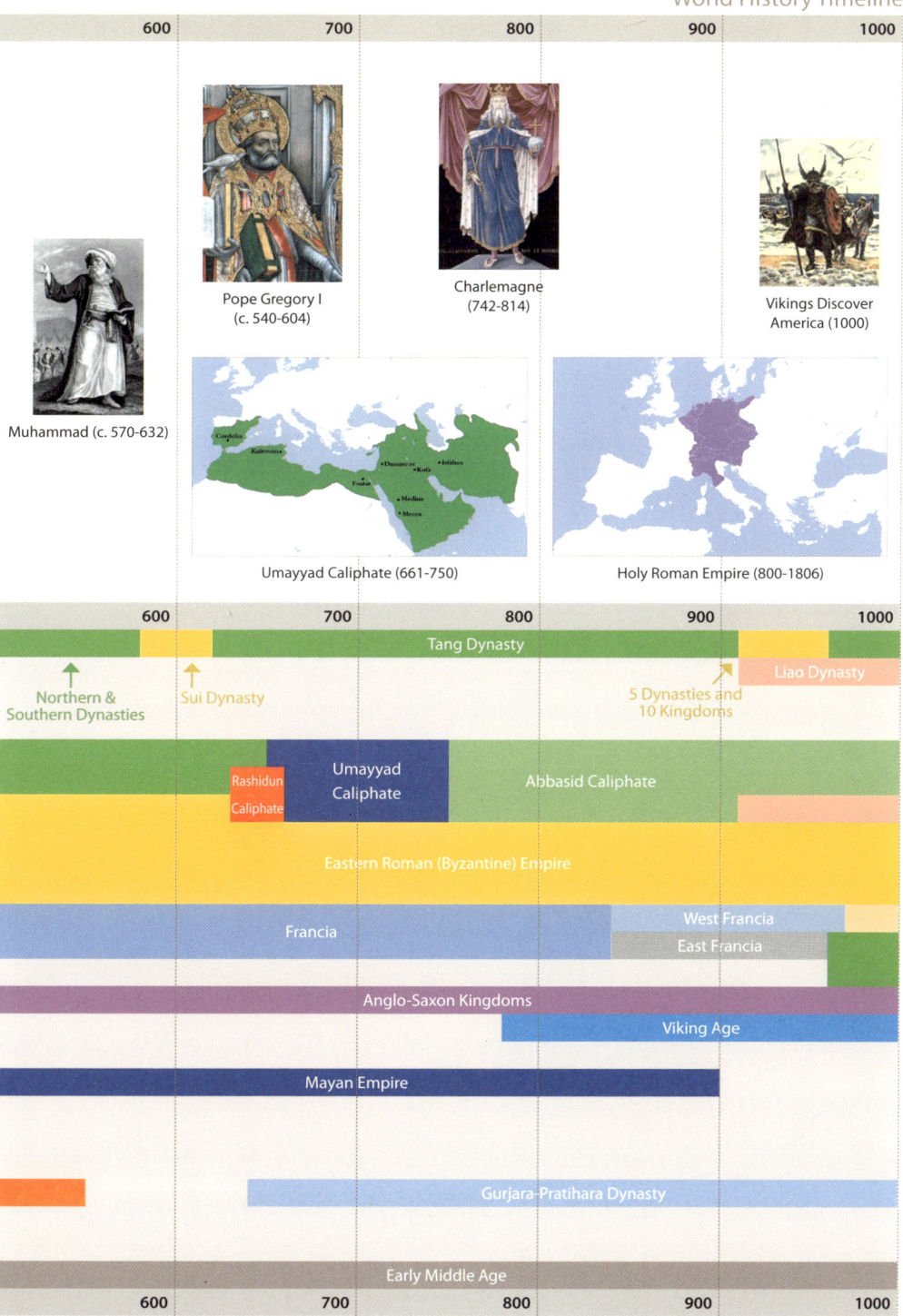

| 600 | 700 | 800 | 900 | 1000 |

Pope Gregory I
(c. 540-604)

Charlemagne
(742-814)

Vikings Discover
America (1000)

Muhammad (c. 570-632)

Umayyad Caliphate (661-750)

Holy Roman Empire (800-1806)

| 600 | 700 | 800 | 900 | 1000 |

Tang Dynasty

Liao Dynasty

Northern &
Southern Dynasties

Sui Dynasty

5 Dynasties and
10 Kingdoms

Rashidun
Caliphate

Umayyad
Caliphate

Abbasid Caliphate

Eastern Roman (Byzantine) Empire

Francia

West Francia

East Francia

Anglo-Saxon Kingdoms

Viking Age

Mayan Empire

Gurjara-Pratihara Dynasty

Early Middle Age

| 600 | 700 | 800 | 900 | 1000 |

World History Timeline

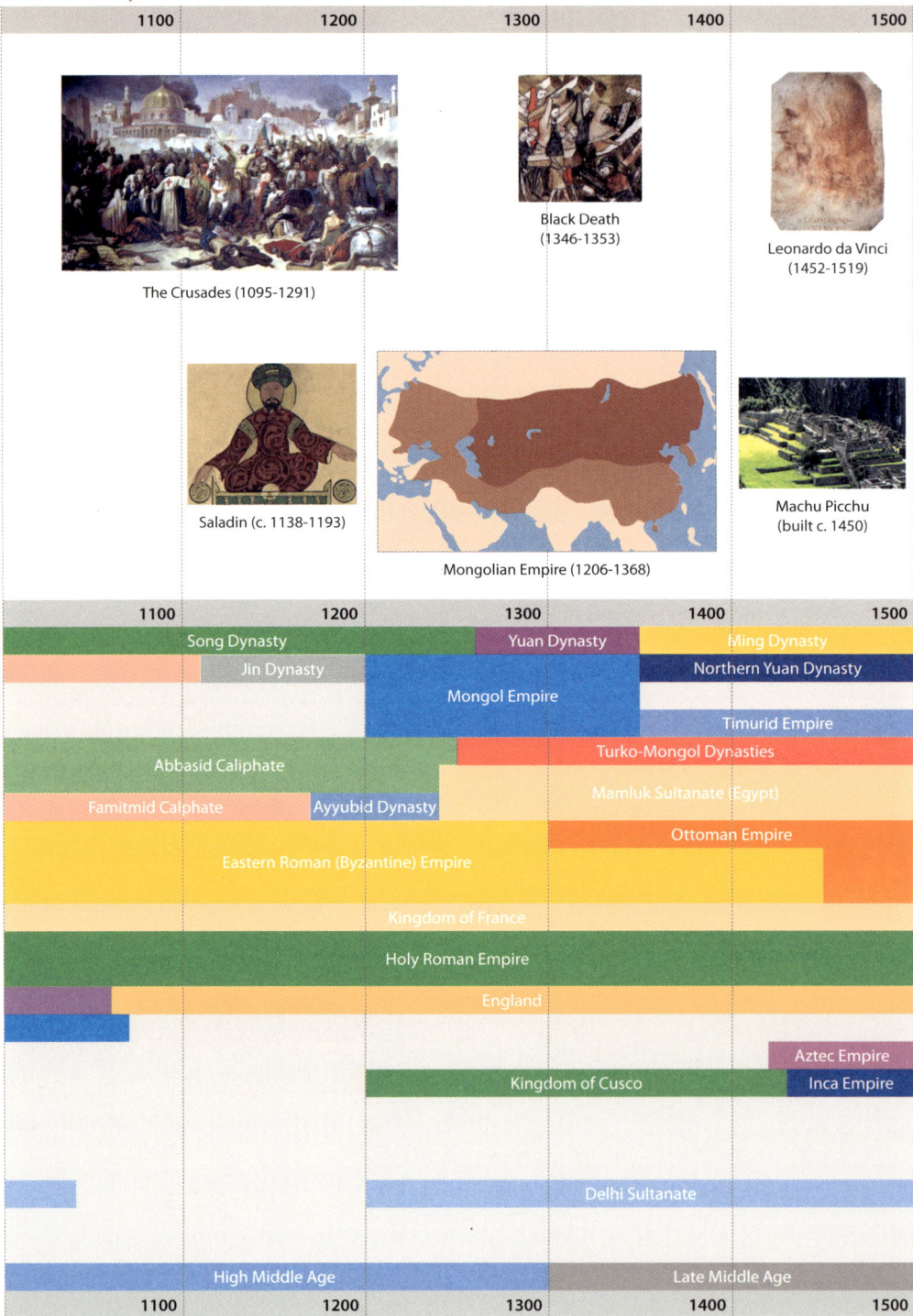

The Crusades (1095-1291)

Black Death (1346-1353)

Leonardo da Vinci (1452-1519)

Saladin (c. 1138-1193)

Mongolian Empire (1206-1368)

Machu Picchu (built c. 1450)

	1100	1200	1300	1400	1500

- Song Dynasty
- Yuan Dynasty
- Ming Dynasty
- Jin Dynasty
- Northern Yuan Dynasty
- Mongol Empire
- Timurid Empire
- Abbasid Caliphate
- Turko-Mongol Dynasties
- Famitmid Calphate
- Ayyubid Dynasty
- Mamluk Sultanate (Egypt)
- Ottoman Empire
- Eastern Roman (Byzantine) Empire
- Kingdom of France
- Holy Roman Empire
- England
- Aztec Empire
- Kingdom of Cusco
- Inca Empire
- Delhi Sultanate
- High Middle Age
- Late Middle Age

	1100	1200	1300	1400	1500